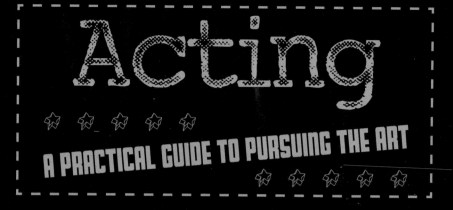

Acting

A PRACTICAL GUIDE TO PURSUING THE ART

BY JASON SKOG

CONTENT ADVISER
Heide Janssen, MFA, Assistant General Manager,
Center Theatre Group, Los Angeles, California

READING ADVISER
Alexa L. Sandmann, EdD, Professor of Literacy,
College and Graduate School of Education, Health, and Human Services,
Kent State University

COMPASS POINT BOOKS
a capstone imprint

Compass Point Books
151 Good Counsel Drive
P.O. Box 669
Mankato, MN 56002-0669

Printed in the United States of America in Stevens Point, Wisconsin.
032010
005741WZF10

Editor: Jennifer Fretland VanVoorst
Designer: Ashlee Suker
Media Researcher: Svetlana Zhurkin
Library Consultant: Kathleen Baxter
Production Specialist: Jane Klenk

Image Credits
Alamy: David Grossman, 34, Greg Ryan, 31, Jim West, 8, 14, 41, Ted Foxx, 9;
Capstone Press/Karon Dubke, 43, 44; Getty Images: Amanda Edwards, 15, David
Livingston, 40, Stone/Emmanuel Faure, 28, UpperCut Images/Michael Grecco, 4;
iStockphoto: Christi Tolbert, 7, Kevin Russ, 21, Michael Krinke, 22, Reuben Schulz,
11; Photo provided by Jason Skog, 18, 27; Shutterstock: Alex Valent, cover (front),
Arena Creative, 38, Dario Diament, 37, haider, 33, kojoku, 20, Lance Bellers, 13,
Marianne Campolongo, 24, Ronald Sumners, cover (background texture) and
throughout, Sean De Burca, 26, Stephen Coburn, 30, Steve Broer, 35, Tatiana
Morozova, 5.

 This book was manufactured with paper containing
at least 10 percent post-consumer waste.

Library of Congress Cataloging-in-Publication Data
Skog, Jason.
  Acting : a practical guide to pursuing the art / by Jason Skog.
    p. cm. — (The performing arts)
  Includes bibliographical references and index.
  ISBN 978-0-7565-4364-8 (library binding)
  1. Acting—Vocational guidance—Juvenile literature.
  I. Title. II. Series.
  PN2055.S66 2011
  792.02'8023—dc22   2010012604

Visit Compass Point Books on the Internet at *www.capstonepub.com*

TABLE OF CONTENTS

You're an Actor

The scene ends, you take a bow, and the crowd roars as the curtain falls. Cameras flash and fans scream as a limo whisks you off to a fancy party to celebrate your amazing performance. Your cell phone rings. Your agent says he's got good news for you. He's gotten you the starring role in the next Hollywood blockbuster.

Beep! Beep! Beep! Is that a car horn? Aw, man. Are we stuck in traffic?

Nope. That's your alarm clock. Time to get up, sleepyhead. It's just another Tuesday morning, and you were only dreaming.

Take a Deep Breath and a Step Back

Whether you're serious about becoming an actor or just curious about acting, it's important to know what it means to be an actor.

Actors are serious professionals who work hard at their craft, transforming themselves into other people for the enjoyment of the audience. They study characters, stories, and roles. They learn how to memorize lines, take direction, and handle criticism.

Many actors never become household names or big Hollywood stars. Some have long stretches between acting roles and have to wait tables or take

You don't need to be a Hollywood star to make a living as an actor.

odd jobs to support themselves.

Actors can find work in a variety of areas, including the theater, television, movies, and the Internet. They appear in commercials, sitcoms, dramas, musicals, romantic comedies, art house films, and variety shows.

They arrived at their positions a number of ways. Some started in school, at a community theater, in a local commercial, or on a dare to audition. Working as an actor takes a combination of hard work, persistence, and luck.

Success varies widely among actors. Some achieve great fame and fortune. Others earn just enough—and sometimes not quite enough—to make a living.

THUMBS UP: WHAT ACTORS ENJOY MOST ABOUT BEING AN ACTOR

It's not hard to guess what actors like most about their jobs. There can be fame, fortune, applause, awards, movie premieres, and fancy parties. Some enjoy the adventure, traveling to exotic locations, and meeting interesting people along the way.

Yet many say what they like most is the work itself. They enjoy the challenge of becoming another person and telling a story—even if they don't win a Tony, Emmy, or Academy Award for it.

But almost all actors have a deep love of acting, and they simply can't see themselves doing anything else.

Important Skills and Qualities

Before stepping on stage, most actors have qualities that made them want to take that step in the first place.

Actors are often outgoing and comfortable being around strangers and speaking in front of large groups. They also enjoy performing and entertaining others.

The best actors have confidence, a positive attitude, and an ability to think on their feet and stay focused when things don't go as planned.

Actors are expressive people who know how to convey meaning and emotion through their voice, body language, and facial expressions.

Chapter 1

Developing Your Skills

Getting Started, Getting Training

Before most actors have appeared on TV, in movies, or on Broadway, they usually have started lower. Much lower. Most actors have worked their way up through various levels of acting and theater. Perhaps they started in a high school play, discovered they liked it, and got a role in a local community theater. From there they moved on to bigger roles in regional theaters or took a shot and moved to Hollywood or New York City.

The path to a career in acting is varied. It can be quick, easy, and direct for some of the lucky ones. For others, the road is long, difficult, and discouraging.

Here's a look at ways to get the education, experience, and opportunity needed to become a working actor.

Student Theater

If you're interested in getting started in acting, there's no better place than in a school play.

Middle schools and high schools often produce a comedy, drama, or musical once or twice (or more) a year.

The Rodgers and Hammerstein musical Oklahoma! *is a popular choice for high school and community theater groups.*

Check with your school's drama department or theater arts program about when and where auditions are held. Some communities offer acting as an after-school activity.

Most actors' first acting part was in a school play. Whether it was the lead role or a bit part, they say the experience had a lasting effect on them. It made them recognize the power of acting and the thrill of the theater.

Many of them continued seeking roles in their schools' productions. That was how they learned how to memorize lines, take direction, handle criticism, and manage stage fright.

Magnet Schools, Private Schools, and Coaches

For serious aspiring actors, some schools are devoted to the study of the performing arts. These schools, often called magnet schools, stage regular theatrical productions and offer classes in acting, singing, and dancing, as well as instruction on technical aspects of theater such as lighting, scenery, and sound.

If you do not have access to a school with an established theater program or there are no theater magnet schools in your area, consider attending a private acting school or hiring an acting coach.

Private acting schools often have programs tailored to students' experience and availability. Some have classes

An actor who is also skilled in singing and dancing is known as a triple threat.

that are just a month long. Others may last a year.

Individual acting coaches are another option. Acting coaches, who typically are actors themselves, can lead group or private classes for those interested in honing their skills.

If you can't find an acting school or coach in your area, you can check out the many resources online. From articles to video tutorials, lectures, and lessons, new acting information is posted on the Internet every day. Try searching for "online acting school" or "acting classes."

LaGuardia High School

The hallways at New York City's Fiorello H. LaGuardia High School are filled with kids who look like most American teenagers. Baggy jeans. Hoodies. Sneakers. Backpacks.

But this isn't your average high school, and these aren't your average students. LaGuardia is the prestigious visual and performing arts school made famous by *Fame*, a 1980s movie and TV show that was recently remade as a movie.

Students at LaGuardia must show an aptitude for acting, singing, or dancing, but it helps to be strong in all three. Although students graduate with academic diplomas, they are also being groomed for careers as professionals or for further study in dance, drama, voice, music, visual arts, or the technical aspects of theater.

LaGuardia's drama department gives students the training they need either to go directly into careers in acting—in theater, film, or television—or to continue with their studies at the college level. Courses include Theatre History and Criticism, Acting, Voice and Diction, Physical Techniques, and Dance: Ballet, Jazz, Tap, and Theatre Dance.

Actors who graduated from LaGuardia High School include Jennifer Aniston, Sarah Michelle Gellar, Adrian Grenier, Al Pacino, and Wesley Snipes.

A lit sign for a theater's stage door is a beacon of welcome for actors.

Other Amateur Theaters

If your school has few plays or is not giving you the experience you seek, consider trying out for roles in productions put on by your local community theater or at churches in your area.

Attend performances by these groups, and stick around after the show to ask the actors or director how you can get involved. Find out how often they put on their productions, and ask when they hold auditions and whether you would be able to try out.

The Web site of the American Association of Community

Students in Detroit, Michigan, have fun performing as part of Mosaic Youth Theater.

Theater also has a directory of community theaters in your area. Visit *www.aact.org* for more information.

Colleges and Universities

Not all professional actors have formal training or a degree in the arts. Some have a natural talent that they have developed through years of experience. But those actors are rare. Many professional actors attended college and earned a degree such as a bachelor of fine arts.

Most colleges and universities have a drama department, though some are especially well known for

Schools with a drama department usually have dedicated performance facilities.

having many theater class offerings and for staging regular, elaborate productions.

Colleges with established drama departments usually have programs that require three to four years of study. These programs concentrate on developing acting skills but often include courses that provide a broader understanding of all areas of the performing arts.

Look Beyond the Lead

So you gave the best audition of your life, and you didn't get the lead role? That doesn't mean you can't still be an actor. Whether it's TV, movies, or the theater, there are plenty of roles for a variety of actors.

METHOD ACTING

Certain actors use certain approaches and techniques when playing a role. The approaches involve lengthy training, discipline, and practice. They are designed to help actors deliver the best, most believable performances possible.

The so-called "method" school of acting was designed by Konstantin Stanislavski in the early 20th century. Developed in his Moscow Arts Theater in Russia, the approach became more popular when it first appeared in New York City in the 1930s. It was expanded and revised by Lee Strasberg in the 1940s.

Method acting requires actors to turn inward and search for a character's mind-set and motivation. They ask themselves what their character wants and why. They even recall moments from their own lives that trigger the emotion they wish to portray.

For example, by remembering the time their dog died, they can better reveal and show grief or sadness. By recalling the time their best friend stole their boyfriend or girlfriend, they can better reveal a character's anger.

Some method actors continue playing a character even while off camera or offstage, even though that is not part of the method approach. Famous method actors include Johnny Depp, Daniel Day-Lewis, Robert De Niro, Jennifer Jason Leigh, Al Pacino, Ellen Burstyn, and Christian Bale.

Remember, there are more actors than there are stars. Beyond the lead, there are many rewarding roles for character actors, supporting actors, ensemble actors, voice actors, and extras.

Character actors: While they might not have familiar names, character actors often have faces you can't forget. They show up time and time again playing a variety of roles. Sometimes they're the bad guy. Sometimes they're a good guy. Sometimes they're completely ordinary. Character actors might not get their name on the Hollywood Walk of Fame, but they often get the most work and have long, stable careers.

Supporting actors: These actors are those who don't have top billing in a movie or play but whose performances support the production. Supporting actors might not draw an audience to a movie or play, but they can be "scene stealers" and deliver performances that you will remember long after leaving the theater.

Ensemble actors: Ensemble actors are part of a large cast of supporting actors. They might appear as a member of the chorus in musical productions with large groups of singers and dancers.

Voice actors: These actors provide the voices for animated characters, radio programs, and voice-overs. They also work as narrators. While they often lack

The Broadway musical Cats *requires a great number of ensemble actors who can also sing and dance.*

recognizable faces, the best voice actors have some of the most versatile and memorable voices you've ever heard.

Extras: These actors are also known as background actors because they appear in the background of movies and plays. They show up just briefly or in passing, usually without even uttering a line. Being an extra still means having to be on stage or set with the rest of the cast. Sometimes extras unexpectedly land a brief speaking role that leads to their big break. Some of Hollywood's biggest stars appeared as extras in their early careers, including Brad Pitt, Renee Zellweger, Sylvester Stallone, Clint Eastwood, and Jackie Chan.

THUMBS DOWN: What Actors Dislike About Their Job

There are so many great things about being an actor, it's hard to imagine there's anything not to like, right? Wrong. Actors everywhere have things they hate about being an actor.

The life of an actor can be unpredictable. They often don't know how long their job will last, how much it will pay them, or whether they'll get another role again.

They also dislike working many hours in a day. For film and TV actors, rehearsals, shooting, and re-shooting can require 12- and 15-hour days on the set. Some projects involve travel to distant places and long stretches away from home and family.

Actors sometimes must deal with freaky and even frightening fan behavior, unflattering reviews from critics, constant battles with celebrity photographers — "paparazzi" — and the struggle to stay fit, attractive, and young looking.

Actor Close-Up

Name: Suzanne Grodner

Age: 50

Hometown: Burlingame, California

Education: BA from San Francisco State University, MFA from Florida State University/ Asolo Conservatory

Notable theater roles:

Dr. Gorgeous in *Sisters Rosensweig*, Miss Bates in *Emma*, Kate in *Broadway Bound*, Dorine in *Tartuffe*, Angel in *Angels in America*, La Carlotta in *Phantom of the Opera*, and Mrs. Frank in *Diary of Anne Frank*; she also appeared on Broadway in *The Rose Tattoo* and *Bye-Bye Birdie*.

What made you want to become an actor? I had an amazing acting teacher in high school who saw something in me and let me know that I had a certain talent, and then nurtured that talent for four years. He gave me an opportunity to be daring on stage, to be daring in class, to try something and fail and have that be OK. He gave me confidence and encouragement, and when I was done with high school, he made sure I continued on to college with other mentors who then continued where he left off. I was lucky. I had some incredible mentors. They set the groundwork for me, and I took that and ran with it.

What was your first acting experience like? Horrible. I was in middle school. The drama club, which I was in, was doing a short play that was to be presented at an assembly for the whole school. I was the lead. I wasn't the most popular gal at the time, and when I walked out on stage, the entire audience first started laughing and then started booing. I was mortified. But I took a breath and kept going. They settled down, and then they started laughing with me instead of at me, and by the end of the play, I was hooked. It was a triumphant moment that I've never forgotten.

What's the best thing about being an actor? The money! OK, seriously, I'd say the best thing for me are the people I get to work with—wonderful, creative, talented, funny, passionate people who love what they do and who can't wait to get up in the morning and go to work. The second best thing for me is the rehearsal process. That's where you make your discoveries about the play and the character, where you collaborate with your director and the other actors you're working with, where you build relationships with this new family in your life.

What advice do you have for kids interested in becoming actors? The best advice I can give you is this: Unless acting is absolutely the only thing you can do in your life that will fulfill you and make you happy, don't go into this profession. Acting takes bravery and tenacity. It's not for the weak of heart. It's filled with rejection, unbelievable competition, frustration, insecurity, and plenty of unemployment. Don't get me wrong; it's also filled with incredible joy and the highest highs imaginable. Also the lowest lows imaginable. It's not for anyone who isn't 100 percent dedicated to their craft.

Chapter 2

Getting Experience, Finding Work

Headshots, Résumés, and Demo Reels

For the experienced amateur actor eager to turn pro, there's a little work to do first. Almost every casting director will ask you to leave a headshot, a résumé, and maybe a demo reel after an audition.

A headshot is an 8-inch by 10-inch (20-centimeter by 25-centimeter) black and white close-up photograph of your face. Casting directors want to remember what you look like and any special features you have. Studio lighting generally works best for a headshot, so check with fashion, portrait, or wedding photographers in your area.

A résumé describes your education and work experience, and lists your vital statistics (age, height, weight, hair color, and eye color), along with ways to contact you or your agent. Some actors include a small photo of themselves on their résumé. Try to limit your résumé to one page, and keep the design clean, organized, and easy to read.

Demo reels are video highlights of your best work. They can show the range of parts you've played and remind directors of your voice and how you carry yourself. Put your demo on a DVD, and try to keep it less than three minutes long.

Hitting the Streets

With a headshot and résumé in hand, you can start looking for an agent, manager, or both to represent you. You're also ready to attend open casting calls.

Established actors with agents often use these open auditions to find suitable roles for which they might try out. For beginners, where they live will largely determine the types of roles they can pursue. Those living in New York City, Hollywood, or Chicago can check trade publications like *Variety*, *The Hollywood Reporter*, and

Actors respond to an open casting call in New York City.

Backstage, which regularly list open casting calls.

But for aspiring actors in other parts of the country, it's catch as catch can. They have to constantly seek out productions in their own cities or places nearby and inquire about auditions.

Local newspapers occasionally list open auditions, and some festival and theater groups have newsletters or Web sites that list auditions. Some theater groups have Web sites that allow you to sign up to get e-mail alerts when new audition opportunities arise.

MONEY, MONEY, MONEY

So you're wondering how much you might get paid after all this? Actor pay varies widely and is very unpredictable, even for those with a hit show or regular gig.

According to a federal study, most actors earned between $8.50 per hour and $22.50 per hour in 2006. The lowest-paid 10 percent earned less than $7.30 an hour, while the highest-paid 10 percent earned more than $51 per hour. The most famous actors—representing a small fraction of all actors—earn much, much more.

The Audition

Auditions are to an actor what job interviews are to the rest of the working world. It is an opportunity for you to present yourself and your skills. It's also a chance for the casting director to decide whether you are right for the part available.

Before the audition, make sure you get a good night's sleep. That day, wear nice-looking but comfortable clothes. Eat a little something and relax.

Some auditions will require you to read for a certain role. If you have received the lines in advance, learn them well. You may be asked to memorize them. Also think about the character delivering the lines. Imagine how he or

Auditions can be nerve-racking. It helps to remember you're not the only one with butterflies in your stomach.

she speaks. Is it loudly or quietly? Fast or slow? Is there an accent? Try to picture what the character would wear and how he or she might walk.

At other auditions you can deliver a monologue of your choosing. A monologue is a solo speaking part, so you are talking on your own without a partner. Printed audition monologues are available online and in bookstores. Pick something that's age appropriate and that doesn't make you stumble or search for words.

Actor Close-Up

Name: Rosie Perez

Age: 45

Hometown: Brooklyn, New York

Education: Two years of college as a biochemistry major

Notable film roles: Tina in *Do The Right Thing*, Gloria in *White Men Can't Jump*, Carla Rodrigo in *Fearless* (for which she was nominated for a supporting actress Academy Award), Cindy in *Untamed Heart*, Muriel Lang in *It Could Happen to You*, Bertha in *Lackawanna Blues*, and Carol in *Pineapple Express*

What made you want to become an actor? I was discovered by [director] Spike Lee in a Los Angeles nightclub. We got into an argument, and he told me, "Tonight is fate." The rest is history.

What was your first acting experience like? My first acting experience was my first movie, *Do The Right Thing*. It was very bittersweet. I had no prior training, let alone any desire to do this, so it was exciting, confusing, and scary. It wasn't the most nurturing of sets to be on, but it was also exhilarating to be a part of the whole magical process of moviemaking.

What's the best thing about being an actor? There are three best things about being an actor for me: giving so much to your audience, living out your passion, and making a living from it as well.

What advice do you have for kids interested in becoming actors? Learn your craft! Work hard. Never give up if this is your true passion. Check your ego at the door. Have fun.

Screen Tests

A screen test is like a final audition for a TV or movie role. You've already impressed the casting director with an audition, but he or she still isn't sure you are perfect for the role.

A screen test lets the director and network or studio executives see how you look on camera with full lighting, makeup, and your hair professionally styled.

If you are being seriously considered for a part, the director may ask you to read lines with actors who have already been cast in the production.

You will probably read lines with actors who are already in the cast.

This gives those who run the show a better feel for how you would come across on screen, which may be different from how you appear in real life.

Callbacks

If the casting director is happy with your audition—or can't decide whether you're right for the role—you might get a callback. While a callback is not a guarantee that you have the job, it means you are still being considered.

A callback is something of a second chance, both for you and for those casting the role. You might receive instruction about how to approach the role or even be asked to read for a different part. Be receptive to their suggestions and feedback, because that will increase your chances of landing a role.

Interviews

In some casting situations, a director will want to interview you. The director may feel you have the look and talent to perform the role, but he or she may have questions about what kind of person you are or what you might be like to work with.

Being interviewed means you are one step closer to getting a role. An interview is less of a performance, but you still have to put forth your best effort. Be prepared to talk about your experience, your skills, the kind of actor you are, and what you hope to become.

Don't be afraid to ask questions. Show interest in the director. Ask how he or she got started, how he or she came

An interview is your chance to impress the director with your poise and professionalism.

to be involved with this production, and what some of his or her favorite performances are. This demonstrates poise and professionalism and shows you are interested in hearing what others have to say—not just hearing yourself talk.

Seasonal Theater Festivals

Summer theater and seasonal productions are staged for just a short time. Typically held in areas that attract summer vacation crowds, these productions must get up and running quickly, and they continue for a short but intense period.

While seasonal theater might seem a natural spot to

break into the business, directors of these productions want serious, committed professionals who can handle the tight deadlines and high expectations. Directors tend not to take a chance on an actor who has only a passing interest in theater.

Still, seasonal theater is an opportunity for a beginning actor to gain valuable professional experience.

Regional Theater

While most acting jobs seem to be in New York City or Los Angeles, there is a thriving theater scene in most large cities in the United States. The cities have a vibrant nightlife and arts and cultural activities where actors can find work without waiting tables.

Cities with strong and successful theater

Actors at the Children's Theater Company in Minneapolis, Minnesota, perform in The Wizard of Oz.

communities include Atlanta, Georgia; Chicago, Illinois; Dallas, Texas; Miami, Florida; Minneapolis and St. Paul, Minnesota; Philadelphia, Pennsylvania; Portland, Oregon; San Francisco, California; Seattle, Washington; and Washington, D.C.

In these cities, actors tend to have less competition for desirable roles, they can establish long-term relationships with theaters and directors, and the lower cost of living often affords them a better lifestyle.

Acting in Commercials

How can a 30-second commercial make you a star? If you do an amazing job or the right person sees you at the right time, you never know what might happen.

For established actors, commercials are a way to fill the time between jobs and earn extra money. For less experienced actors, commercials are a way to

Young Actors and Child Labor Laws

There are strict laws about children in the workplace, and they are no different for young actors. Federal and state laws limit the hours young people can work and include safety, supervision, and schooling requirements. Check with your state's labor division or the U.S. Department of Labor Web site if you have questions.

Competition for commercial roles can be stiff, but they are a good way to break into the business.

break into acting and help pay the bills.

Commercials can be straightforward product promotions or productions with more complicated or ongoing storylines. They can also be a lot of work. Shooting big-budget commercials can take many hours over many days, sometimes in uncomfortable conditions, such as extreme heat or cold.

Competition for landing a commercial role can be stiff. Companies are very careful about whom they choose to be the face of their business.

New York City's Broadway district is jam-packed with theatrical productions of every kind.

Acting on Broadway

Perhaps no other kind of acting delivers a reward as immediate as performing in a Broadway play.

The audience is right there in front of you, following your every word and action. They laugh, smile, and cry along with the actors. At the curtain, they may erupt with loud applause and cheers and give the cast a standing ovation.

Broadway actors experience that joy night in and night out—and twice on Wednesdays and Saturdays, if there's a matinee show.

The rigorous work schedule is what makes being on Broadway such a challenge. Actors must be prepared to deliver a strong performance night after night and keep it as fresh as it was on opening night.

It's not easy, but for actors who have the skill and nerve to pull it off, nothing else compares.

Acting on TV

The variety of acting jobs on television is as great as the variety of shows and channels.

But television basically has two categories of programs:

Actors rehearse a scene from the hit TV series Law and Order.

episodic and half-hour. Episodic shows are usually an hour long with storylines that continue from week to week. Half-hour programs include most comedies.

Landing a role on a regular TV series is one of acting's greatest rewards. The money can be tremendous, and the exposure can springboard you into other good jobs.

The work can feel repetitive. Same set. Same characters. Same co-workers. But each week presents a fresh batch of challenges: new lines to learn, directions to take, characters to introduce, or locations to visit.

Acting in the Movies

While actors might argue about the various merits of TV, theater, and film, the public has given movie actors— particularly movie stars—special status.

Whether it's because of the big screen, the glitzy awards shows, the massive paychecks, or the sweeping sagas in which they appear, Hollywood stars have an uncommon appeal. It's also what many young people dream about becoming when they first think about being an actor.

The work of a movie actor varies depending on the role, the movie's budget, and the actors and crew surrounding them. Jobs can be challenging, rewarding, boring, or thrilling. The most successful actors adapt to these situations and deliver the best performance possible.

BEHIND THE SCENES AT A FEATURE FILM

There's controlled chaos on a movie set. Dozens of people scurry about the brightly lit, colorful soundstage. It's a jumble of cameras, lights, cables, microphones, monitors, and props, yet everybody knows where to be and what to do.

People take orders over walkie-talkies, touch up the actors' hair and makeup, and give last-minute instructions before the next shot. The actors take their positions as the director says "Action!"

The music thumps, and the actors dance and sing in a particularly silly scene. The crew tries to keep from laughing and ruining the take. In the end, the director likes the take and says, "That's a wrap." The crew applauds. It's the end of a long day.

Time for an Agent?

If going to audition after audition feels a bit like running on a treadmill, perhaps it's time you hired an agent.

Agents can help you line up auditions for the roles most appropriate for you. They have contacts in the industry and can help you cut through the clutter and give you a better shot at landing a role.

But finding an agent can feel like an audition itself. The fact that you want an agent doesn't mean the agent wants you. Some already have all the clients they can handle. Others only accept established actors.

An agent can help you with the business aspects of acting so you are free to concentrate on your art.

Check out the Association of Talent Agents for a list of agents and agencies. The ATA is a nonprofit organization whose members represent more than 90 percent of the actors working in Hollywood and New York.

Paying Your (Union) Dues

For most professional actors, membership in a union comes with the job. Companies with union contracts aren't allowed to hire nonunion workers except in rare or first-time circumstances.

Three unions cover just about all actors and performers. The Screen Actors Guild—SAG for short—represents actors who appear in film and television.

The American Federation of Television and Radio Artists represents actors who do live and taped TV shows, soap operas, commercials, and radio broadcasts. AFTRA membership is available to actors, singers, dancers, announcers, disc jockeys, talk-show hosts, stunt people, sportscasters, and journalists.

The Actors Equity Association, better known as simply Equity, covers performers and stage managers in the theater.

Members have to pay an initiation fee and regular dues to get the protections and benefits the unions provide.

Actor Close-Up

Name: Jerry Trainor

Age: 32

Hometown: San Diego, California

Education: BFA in acting from the University of California, Santa Barbara

Notable TV roles: Spencer on *iCarly*, Crazy Steve on *Drake and Josh*, and Brian the AV Guy on *Crossing Jordan*; also appeared in *Malcolm in the Middle* and the film *Donnie Darko*.

What made you want to become an actor?
My insatiable need for attention. Kidding—sort of. Actually I learned at a very young age that I love—LOVE—to make an audience laugh. We would do skits in grade school, and once I got a taste of audience feedback, I knew I needed more. In the process, I discovered I had a knack for physical comedy, which is great because it's what I love to watch as well.

What was your first acting experience like? My first professional acting experience was nerve-racking because I was new to Los Angeles, and when you're new, every job feels like your entire career is riding on your performance. I couldn't eat, I didn't know where to be or how to behave— just total nervousness. The nerves went away once we started rolling and I could hear the laughs in the back; it became fun, less pressure.

What's the best thing about being an actor? Gold planes that land on the roof of my giant mansion and take me to my very own golden 7-Eleven for beef jerky and caviar. Seriously. I'm not joking.

What advice do you have for kids interested in becoming actors?
Persevere. If you truly love it and you get a sense that people want to see you do it, then never give up. Success in artistry is a weird mixture of talent, timing, and a little luck thrown in. But if you keep going and enjoy the ups and downs and create your own opportunities, then your time will come.

Learning Your Lines

All actors are expected to memorize their lines. They need to know their parts—and the parts of other actors who appear in the scenes they do—backward and forward.

Learning how to learn lines is a special skill. Some actors are better than others, but "running lines" is the method most actors use. After reading and re-reading your part, find a parent or a friend willing to read the parts of the other characters in the scene while you read your part.

As you run lines, you will learn what lines come before

TAKING DIRECTION

The director is in charge of the entire film, TV, or theater production. He or she oversees the look and feel of the production and how the performers play their parts.

Most directors know how they want a character to come across, based on the script or screenplay. If the actor is struggling to deliver that performance, it's up to the director to step in. So even if you think you know all there is to know about your craft and your character, listen to the director's input.

The director might talk about what your character is feeling at that point in the story or what your character might be thinking about another character. The director works to make an actor's words and actions authentic and believable.

yours and how you should react to what other characters are saying.

Practice Makes Perfect

Every play, TV, or film production puts actors through rehearsals before the show begins. The practice performances help actors go through their lines and learn how to interact with others in each scene. They also learn blocking, the term for an actor's movements on stage or in a scene. Blocking tells them how to enter a scene, where to stand, how to move, what to do, and when and how to leave.

Rehearsals also help those behind the scenes learn their jobs in the production. Lighting designers, stagehands, and wardrobe and makeup departments all need rehearsal time.

Opening Night Jitters

If you're nervous before your first performance, don't worry. It's normal.

Actors usually rehearse in everyday clothes, but they will change into costumes for rehearsals as the big day approaches.

Most actors say that the first time they stepped on a stage, they were so nervous they thought they might throw up. Some actually did! But they also said that once the performance began, their nervousness disappeared and the time passed so fast they barely remember the show.

If somebody tells you to break a leg just as you're about to step on stage, don't get mad. The person is trying to do you a favor. An old acting superstition suggests it's actually bad luck to wish somebody good luck.

Final Advice

Becoming an actor and making a living at it are not easy, and acting is not for everyone. It takes hard work, energy, talent, and more than a bit of good fortune. Of all the actors who have stepped on stage or appeared on screen, only a small number have achieved great riches or recognition.

If you have carefully considered

Acting can be an incredibly rewarding profession. What other job lets you try on other people's lives for a living?

the idea of an acting career, honestly assessed yourself and your skills, and discussed your goals with your parents or guardians and trusted friends, it's time to make your move.

Action!

Whether it's trying out for the school play or church musical, taking a course at your community college, or auditioning

Supporting Cast

Beyond the support of family and friends, actors need a large supporting cast to break into the business and keep working. They have agents who help them find their next role, personal managers who help them make career decisions, business managers who take care of money matters, and publicists who work to get their name in the media and promote their latest projects. For young actors, parents might fill some or all of these positions until a child's career takes off.

alongside dozens of other hopefuls, it's time to act.

If you don't get a part or things didn't go your way, consider whether you truly did your best and even whether the role was right for you. Remember: There are plenty of roles for those who aren't the star of the show. And if you realize acting isn't what you had hoped it would be, there are many other rewarding careers in the field.

Good luck. Actually, break a leg!

GLOSSARY

audition   short performance by an actor to see whether he or she is suitable for a part in a play, TV show, or film

blocking   actor's movements on stage or in a scene

casting   selecting actors for a play, TV show, or film

demo reel   video recording of highlights of an actor's best work

headshot   8-inch by 10-inch (20-centimeter by 25-centimeter) black and white close-up photograph of an actor's face

monologue   long speech by one person

ovation   audience response with loud applause and cheering

persistence   continuing an effort with determination regardless of obstacles

résumé   brief list of a person's jobs, education, and awards

rigorous   demanding and challenging

screen test   filmed audition that shows how an actor will appear on screen

storylines   tales that continue from one episode to the next

take   scene filmed at one time without stopping the camera

unflattering   something that makes you look bad

versatile   being able to do many things or adapt to new situations

vibrant   exciting and lively

READ MORE

Belli, Mary Lou, and Dinah Lenney. *Acting for Young Actors: The Ultimate Teen Guide*. New York: Back Stage Books, 2006.

Kenney, Karen Latchana. *Cool Scripts and Acting: How to Stage Your Very Own Show*. Edina, Minn.: ABDO Pub. Company, 2010.

Martin, Rod. *Drama Games and Acting Exercises: 177 Games and Activities*. Colorado Springs, Colo.: Meriwether Pub., 2009.

Mayfield, Katherine. *Acting A to Z: The Young Person's Guide to a Stage or Screen Career*. New York: Back Stage Books, 2007.

INTERNET SITES

FactHound offers a safe, fun way to find Internet sites related to this book. All of the sites on FactHound have been researched by our staff.

Here's all you do:

Visit *www.facthound.com*

Type in this code: 9780756543648

INDEX

About the Author

Jason Skog is a freelance writer and author of many books for young readers. He lives with his wife and two young sons in Brooklyn, New York.